a former teenage girl

Love Letters

To

God

From a Teenage Girl

a former teenage girl

Love Letters

To

God

From a Teenage Girl

By

Minister Onedia N. Gage

Purple Ink Press
Houston, TX

a former teenage girl

DEDICATION

To ALL teenage girls

(current and former):

May God continue to bless your journey. May you be sensitive to His voice, touch and guidance.

May these words reach and empower and touch and affect, may these words strengthen you and help you reach some resolve. May you be inspired to achieve your goals and dreams. May you enhance your relationship with God so that your other relationships will also improve. May you enhance your self-esteem through prayer and studying. May you have courage and peace. Share love the best you can until you can share love without reservation.

To my girl, my daughter: Hillary! I pray your strength each day. Remember that God's love is the most important love! God is your strong tower. Seek Him! I hope I have modeled that journey for you! I love you!

a former teenage girl

THE WORD

Trust

In God I have but my trust, I shall not be afraid. What can man do to me?

Psalm 56:11 (NIV)

Hope

Trust steadily in God, hope unswervingly, love extravagantly.

1 Corinthians 13:13 (MSG)

Love

But God demonstrates His own love toward us, in that while we were yet sinners, Christ died for us.

Romans 5:8 (NIV)

a former teenage girl

OTHER BOOKS BY
ONEDIA N. GAGE

As We Grow Together Daily Devotional for Expectant Couples

As We Grow Together Prayer Journal for Expectant Couples

The Blue Print: Poetry for the Soul

In Purple Ink: Poetry for the Spirit

Living An Authentic Life

The Measure of a Woman: The Details of Her Soul

On This Journey Daily Devotional for Young People

On This Journey Prayer Journal for Young People

One More Day Than We Deserve Daily Devotional

One More Day Than We Deserve Prayer Journal

Promises, Promises: A Novel

Yielded and Submitted: A Woman's Journey for a Life Dedicated to God

Library of Congress

Love Letters to God

From a Teenage Girl

All Rights Reserved © 2012

Onedia N. Gage

Purple Ink, Inc. Press

For Information address:

Purple Ink, Inc

P O Box 41232

Houston, TX 77241

www.purpleink.net

www.onediagage.com

ISBN:

978-1-939119-00-1

Printed in United States

TABLE OF CONTENTS

a former teenage girl

Dear Teenage Girl:

Greetings! You are a diva and a diamond. You are a daughter. Diamonds are found in mines—in dark, dangerous, unreachable places indeed. They are found inside coal—black, dense, and tough. As the diamond is uncovered, it does not have the shape found in stores. It is large and shapeless, and valuable. Its value is based on potential rather than actual. So when the gemologist shapes the diamond, the goal is to shape the diamond with the ultimate clarity and the clearest of colors so that it will give off the most brilliance, these have the highest value.

Unlike diamonds, we were not birthed in darkness. We know we were designed to be excellent. We have just managed to abandon the plan—God's plan. God will shape you into the diamond He desires, with the amount of brilliance He deserves, and the ultimate excellence. These words are designed to help you avoid these dark, damp places. His guidance makes the difference. Our obedience makes the difference. His love guarantees the difference.

As your journey of becoming God's best work continues, I pray these letters and journal help you. I pray that they stir your heart for a closer and more intimate relationship with God, Jesus and the Holy Spirit.

God has plans, specific plans, for your life and has had them since He decided to form you in your mother's womb. God's will is for those plans to be executed and be a reality. God certainly keeps His promises and always wants His will to be done.

Diamond, stay focused on God, pray without ceasing, and remain in His arms. I can't wait to hear all about your journey. onediagage@onediagage.com. Via Twitter @onediangage.

Diva is defined as an elegant lady who is respected and wise and considered a dynamic person. In this role as DIVA, you are growing into the calling on your life. This season is for growth as you continue to understand yourself through God's eyes and His word.

Each love letter has two parts: the love letter and the journal. The journal is used for all reflections, prayers and promises which the letters and the Scriptures inspire.

Journaling provides the script for growth. Journaling gives you a moment to digest and decompress about your journey. Later in your journey, you are able to reflect on your past, consequently your growth.

Prayer feeds your soul. Prayer is a two-way communication between you and God. Prayer builds relationship and maintains relationship with God. Prayer shares your heart with God. Prayer provides us with God's attention and His instruction. Prayer is the rectification and ratification of sin through relationship. Prayer offers a safe place for God to rescue us. God saves us from ourselves through prayer.

I hope you enjoy this journey through Love Letters to God.

To God be the glory,

Minister Onedia N. Gage

Former Teenager

af·fir·ma·tion

[af-er-mey-shuhn] noun

1. the act or an instance of <u>affirming</u>; state of being <u>affirmed</u>.
2. the assertion that something exists or is true.
3. something that is <u>affirmed</u>; a statement or proposition that is declared to be true.

af·firm

[uh-furm] verb (used with object)

1. to state or assert positively; maintain as true: to affirm one's loyalty to one's country; He affirmed that all was well.
2. to confirm or ratify: The appellate court affirmed the judgment of the lower court.
3. to assert solemnly: He affirmed his innocence.

a former teenage girl

Journal Instructions

Journaling provides the script for growth. Journaling gives you a moment to digest and decompress about your journey. Later in your journey, you are able to reflect on your past, consequently your growth.

There is a space for you to journal on the facing page of the letter. Journaling is an important process of your growth. Empower yourself to share with God all that you have on my mind and heart and soul. Take your time through this process.

As you write in your journal, please consider the following questions:

1. How did the letter speak to you?

2. How are you challenged in this area?

3. What are you believing God for?

4. What are you praying for?

a former teenage girl

Dear My Awesome God:

To My Most Amazing Father and Savior!

I write to You with all that I am and mostly with what I am not. I use my voice (in writing) to share with You what You already know. Thank You for being God and for the gifts You have given me.

Lord, I pray Your blessings over those whose eyes will pass over this page. Breathe Your will and favor in their lives right now, Dear God. Let them know that You are right there holding them together in their greatness and their storms.

We girls need You, God. And we eagerly anticipate Your response to our letters and thoughts.

I love You!

In Your Service,

Onedia N. Gage

Former Teenager

a former teenage girl

The Love Letters

a former teenage girl

Deuteronomy 6:5

"Love the Lord your God with all your heart and with all your soul and with all your strength."

Deuteronomy 6:5

"Love the Lord your God with all your heart and with all your soul and with all your strength."

Father God, today I will love You better than yesterday. I will love You with my whole heart. I won't make You share my love with other people today. Lord, my love for You is growing daily as I understand You better. God, You deserve my love—my dedicated, committed, uninterrupted, pure love.

Father God, today I will search for more ways to commit to You and deepen my relationship with You. You deserve my whole heart, my soul and my strength. I will love You through my situations and my drama.

Lord, today, I will submit my heart, my soul and my strength to You.

Lord, I pray You keep my heart, my soul and my mind for Your use.

Jeremiah 29:11

"For I know the plans I have for you," declares the Lord, "plans to prosper you and not to harm you, plans to give you hope and a future."

Jeremiah 29:11

"For I know the plans I have for you," declares the Lord, "plans to prosper you and not to harm you, plans to give you hope and a future."

God, thank You for having infinite plans and thoughts for my life. God, Your plans for my life are ordained to keep me close to You. God, thank You for investing Your time and Your thoughts in me.

God, thank You for prospering me, especially my soul and my spiritual thirst. God, I want to please You and do not want to disappoint You. Your plans are above all I can imagine and sometimes understand.

God, thank You for hope. Your hope strengthens me and keeps me. Hope is hard to capture yet necessary and meaningful. I want to be able to exercise Your hope in my life. Thank You for this hope offering. Thank You for the promises we have from You.

Thank You, God for Your direction in my life. I love You.

Isaiah 55:8-9

[8] "For My thoughts are not your thoughts, neither are your ways My ways," declares the Lord. [9] "As the heavens are higher than the earth, so are My ways higher than your ways and My thoughts than your thoughts."

Isaiah 55:8-9

[8]*"For My thoughts are not your thoughts, neither are your ways My ways,"* *declares the Lord.* [9]*"As the heavens are higher than the earth, so are My ways higher than your ways and My thoughts than your thoughts."*

God, my thoughts are extremely limited. They certainly do not compare to Your thoughts. God, I wish to surrender my thoughts to You along with my heart, soul, mind, and energy. I owe You God my thoughts, at a dedicated level to You so that I may bring You glory, honor and praise.

God as You have established the heavens for our next dwelling, God, I will praise, worship and honor You. God, thank You for making me see the path You have established for me.

Thank You for an example of great behavior and the reason to abandon my pettiness and foolishness. God, thank You for the inspiration to move forward with my life.

Lord, thank You for the love, the inexhaustible love, You have for me.

a former teenage girl

Exodus 20:2

I am the Lord Your God who brought you out of Egypt, out of the land of slavery.

Exodus 20:2

I am the Lord Your God who brought you out of Egypt, out of the land of slavery.

Lord, thank You for claiming me. There are others who have disowned me who should claim me but won't. Thank You for keeping me close to You. Lord, thank You for loving me in spite of my mistakes, my failures, and not because of my successes, my dreams and my image. Thank You for not casting me away from You regardless of me. Thank You for not ignoring me. Thank You for recognizing my struggle and my pain. Thank You for delivering me from my pain and my suffering. Thank You for delivering me from my enemies.

Thank You for trusting me enough to release me from my "slavery" and my addictions to experience the freedom of Your love and that which You have designed for me. Thank You for the testimony my release prompts in the glory You deserve.

Thank You for being my God. My God of hope. My God of life. My God of love. My God of blessings. My God of rest.

Lord, thank You for not forgetting me in my struggle

a former teenage girl

Exodus 20:3

You shall have no other gods before me.

Exodus 20:3

You shall have no other gods before me.

Thank You for being a great God. God help me focus on Your greatness and Your goodness. Lord allow me to remember that You are first. Lord, I know that it is easy for me to use other people, places and things to be before You. Lord, I apologize for putting other things and people in front of You.

Lord, help me prioritize my life around You. Lord, help me discover Your calling for my life. Lord, bring my sensitivity for You into full focus. The Lord, I want to be so sensitive to Your voice, Your call, and Your desires for me. Lord, keep me focused on You so that I don't accidentally or purposely put something else in front of You.

Thank You Lord, for establishing You as my God, so that I have a guide, a leader and a priority. Let our relationship be an example to others. Father, I pray I remain faithful to You.

Lord, thank You for establishing the boundaries and guidelines in our relationship.

a former teenage girl

Exodus 20:12

Honor your father and your mother, so that you may live long in the land the Lord Your God is giving you.

Exodus 20:12

Honor your father and your mother, so that you may live long in the land the Lord Your God is giving you.

Lord, You gave me a father and mother to help You guide and discipline me. They are important in my life because You chose them for me. When I honor them, I honor and obey You. My obedience is my love for You. Christ, help me to remain obedient.

Lord, as I honor them, please help me with wisdom in this relationship. My parents can sometimes be very difficult. They don't explain everything so I don't understand why I am required to do some of what they say. Lord, please help me communicate at a level pleasing to You. My mother doesn't listen to me but allow me to remain respectful of her. My father doesn't always respond the way I want him to. Please allow me to forgive him when he disappoints me. I know that You are working on all of us. Please watch over us.

Lord, I want us to grow as a family no matter what our circumstances are or become. Remind me that they are human and they make mistakes. Remind me to forgive them. Remind me to love them regardless of their actions or attitudes. Lord Jesus, I thank You for providing me with the land. Your provision to me is gracious and I love You for it.

2 Chronicles 7:14

If My people, who are called by My name, will humble themselves and pray and seek My face and turn from their wicked ways, then I will hear from heaven and will forgive their sin and will heal their land.

2 Chronicles 7:14

If My people, who are called by My name, will humble themselves and pray and seek My face and turn from their wicked ways, then I will hear from heaven and will forgive their sin and will heal their land.

Lord God, thank You for calling me to You and Your service. Lord, help me with remain humble. You are so gracious. You are so worthy of my total commitment to You. I am usually not humble when I have achieved more than expected. Lord God, I dearly want to be humble in Your sight.

Lord, I will pray more consistently. I long for the filling of me with You. I will pray more diligently to You Lord because I know that the intimacy between us is important and something I thirst for. I need You and I need this communication with You so I can understand what You have called me to do, Your unconditional love for me and the relationship You designed for us.

Lord, seeking Your face is one area where I am learning. Lord, I want to please You and be closer to you. If I seek You, I know that You will help me with the sin that approaches me. Thank You for the healing and forgiveness. I thank You for giving us clear guidelines on how to follow You and what You require of us.

Proverbs 3:5-6

⁵ Trust in the Lord with all your heart and lean not on your own understanding. ⁶ In all your ways acknowledge Him and he will direct your path.

Proverbs 3:5-6

[5] *Trust in the Lord with all your heart and lean not on your own understanding.* [6] *In all your ways acknowledge Him and he will direct your path.*

Teach me how to trust You, Lord. In this world, where so much distrust exists, I need help with trusting You. I need help with discerning others who mean harm to me. Lord, I want to trust You with all of my heart: With my whole heart! With all that I am, I want to trust You. I know that my family trusts You and my church friends trust You but I want to trust You!

Lord, help me to disregard my diluted and finite knowledge. Lord, I know that You are the author and creator of everything. Help me to fully depend on You, at all times and in all situations. No matter what!

Lord, thank You for giving me direction and for Your will in my life. Help me recognize it better Lord God than ever before as I face obstacles.

I love You, Lord.

a former teenage girl

Psalm 46:1

God is our refuge and strength, and ever-present help in trouble.

Psalm 46:1

God is our refuge and strength, and ever-present help in trouble.

God as my shelter, my refuge, remind me that I do not have to do anything without You. Thank You for the provision of refuge and shelter from the inevitable storms. Lord, as I learn to view You as shelter, keep watch over my attitude and my timing. I do not want to get ahead of You.

God as with Your complete provision, the consistent help during all my troubles is a comfort to me. I consider Your comfort, protection and love a gift. One I do not deserve.

Thank You for the assurance that You will always be there.

Lord, thank You for Your attention to me.

Psalm 46:10

Be still and know that I am God; I will be exalted among the nations, I will be exalted in the earth.

Psalm 46:10

Be still and know that I am God; I will be exalted among the nations, I will be exalted in the earth.

Lord, I am working on being still. I do not understand the value of that yet. I do know that You are my God. That I am sure of. I know that You are a real God and You understand me and my needs.

As I consider exalting You, I think about my life and will further understand that You are God and You deserve my praise. I keep Your words and promises and You have protected and provided for me.

I know that You have prepared Your earth to exalt, to worship You. I will do better about exalting You and sharing with others Your words.

♦ 43 ♦

a former teenage girl

Psalm 119:105

Your word is a lamp to my feet and a light for my path.

Psalm 119:105

Your word is a lamp to my feet and a light for my path.

Your word is a lamp to my feet means that You gave me Your word so that I would have some direction in this broken world. I need that direction and encouragement in this bleak, hard world. The people around me make me concerned if I am going to be successful. The teachers are not really encouraging me to succeed or to dream.

Thank You for Your direction.

The light for my path where my feet rest is a great companion for the lamp. The light provides the lamp illumination. This couple: the direction and the light for my path.

Thank You for the lamp and the light.

a former teenage girl

Psalm 117:2 KJV

For His loving kindness is great toward us. And the truth of the Lord is everlasting. Praise the Lord!

Psalm 117:2 KJV

For His loving kindness is great toward us. And the truth of the Lord is everlasting. Praise the Lord!

Your loving kindness is so huge. When I hear about Your love for others, I look at my life and realize that love me like that too. You love me more than I understand. Your love covers us—completely and totally.

Your love is the best love we will ever know and experience. Truth is hard to come by in this time in our country. God, thank You for establishing Your truth as standard. It is hard to be totally truthful. I do not want to hurt the feelings of others. I thank You for sharing Your truth with me. Your truth has grown me up and I am sure that I will grow more.

Praise to You my Lord!

a former teenage girl

Psalm 103:1 KJV

Bless the Lord, O My Soul. And all that is within me, bless His holy name.

Psalm 103:1 KJV

Bless the Lord, O My Soul. And all that is within me, bless His holy name.

How do I bless You, Lord? Through my words? My actions? My attitude? How I treat my mother? How I treat my father? How I perform in school? How I clean my room? How I wear my clothes? How I respond when someone angers me? How I act when someone hates me? How I manage the gifts You have given me? How I manage my money? How I decide on what I should do?

I can and will BLESS You in ALL those ways! Thank You for Your gifts and who I am. God, my soul belongs to You. All that I am, God, belongs to You. I commit my soul to You, God. I know that I need to be more committed to my gifts and sharing them for Your glory.

Your name is Holy, God. God, I love You just because I have sung that song and my grandmother said to love You. I am growing each day to love You because I am getting to know You. I give You all of me.

a former teenage girl

Psalm 103:2 KJV

Bless the Lord, O my soul, and forget none of His benefits.

Psalm 103:2 KJV

Bless the Lord, O my soul, and forget none of His benefits.

Lord, if I make a list of all that You have done for me then I cannot forget You.

My family.

My clothes.

My material possessions.

My pet.

My home.

My intelligence.

My school.

My mentors.

My church.

Thank You for keeping my soul safe. I cannot forget how You love me. I cannot forget that You provide for my needs. I cannot forget that You chose me and created everything about me. Lord, You made me beautiful! I won't ever forget—Your forgiveness.

a former teenage girl

Psalm 103:3 KJV

Who pardons all your iniquities; who heals all your diseases.

Psalm 103:3 KJV

Who pardons all your iniquities; who heals all your diseases.

God, You forgive me of all of my wrong doing. Everything I do is not good. You recognize that I need You and Your forgiveness in order to live properly. You are the only one who can save me from myself. Lord, thank You for helping me avoid trouble, temptation and turmoil.

Healing comes from You! Only from You, can I be healed. I need healing from emotional illness and distractions, from physical illnesses and ailments, and mental distractions which come to find myself away from You.

Thank You for not forgetting me. Thank You for keeping me close. Thank You for forgiving me. Thank You for showing me how to forgive others and myself.

Psalm 103:4 KJV

Who redeems your life from the pit; who crowns you with loving kindness and compassion.

Psalm 103:4 KJV

Who redeems your life from the pit; who crowns you with loving kindness and compassion.

God when I realized that You had redeemed me from my sins and my foolishness. I realize that means I could have been somewhere else. I could have fallen on my face or my laurels. You saved my life from the originally planned downfall. You saved me in order to give You glory, Oh God.

I am designed to worship You God with all of who I am—the servant You saved. I am designed to bring God my best work—the best of who I am.

Your loving kindness and compassion toward me is immeasurable. God, I know You love me. You love me with compassion and Your loving kindness. Thank You for continuing to love me. God, I know that it is hard to love me sometimes; okay, most of the time. The weight of Your love and kindness is what keeps me focused on You.

Thank You Lord for meeting my needs.

a former teenage girl

Psalm 103:10 KJV

He has not dealt with us according to our sins, nor rewarded us according to our iniquities.

Psalm 103:10 KJV

He has not dealt with us according to our sins, nor rewarded us according to our iniquities.

God, there was punishment that I deserved when I disrespected my mother, my grandmother, and my leaders. I deserved Your wrath and Your judgment and Your distance. I deserved Your frown and Your tears.

But You didn't. You dealt with me graciously—WAY better than I deserved. You loved on me in an unbelievable, unprecedented, remarkable and outstanding way. I doubt I even love myself as deeply.

Thank You for not giving me what I deserved yet You were forgiving and merciful and outrageously kind to me. You do this each day; each hour and every situation in my life.

Lord, thank You! Help me treat others the same.

Psalm 100:1—2 KJV

¹ Shout joyfully to the Lord, all the Earth. ² Serve the Lord with gladness;

Come before Him with joyful singing.

Psalm 100:1—2 KJV

¹ Shout joyfully to the Lord, all the Earth. ² Serve the Lord with gladness; Come before Him with joyful singing.

I have never shouted to You. I think it means that I tell you in my most authentic voice that I love You, God. I think it means in my most authentic behavior that I love You, God. I want You to know that I love You completely but I may not know how to do it well. Help me to love You better.

I don't know how to serve You. I know to read the Bible—Your word. I know I need to pray. I do sometimes. I want to pray more. Life is hard sometimes and I know I that I NEED You. I am glad that You are my God.

God, I know that You love me. I know that I love being in Your presence. I am learning my voice with You—to praise You, to love You and to serve You.

Psalm 100:3 KJV

Know that the Lord Himself is God; It is He who has made us, and not we

ourselves, we are His people and the sheep of His pasture.

Psalm 100:3 KJV

Know that the Lord Himself is God; It is He who has made us, and not we ourselves, we are His people and the sheep of His pasture.

Knowing that You are God is easy because there is so much evidence. You are demonstrative in Your love for us. We are a destructive people and we are destroying Your work. The evidence is there. The proper amount of oxygen and oil and water is what You supply. We cannot make any of these resources ourselves. The evidence is so obvious.

You made me! You created me and You know each hair on my head. You know my thoughts. I did not make myself. I did not make me. I do not make any thing. I can only do what You allow for me to do and to have.

I am Your people. I was made to be on Your side. I was made to defend Your words. I was made to share You with others. God of excellence.

As Your sheep, I am considering what I need to be the best sheep possible. The ability to follow, the ability to stay with the group and the ability to move with the group are all details that I need to master to be a better sheep.

Thank You Lord!

Psalm 100:4 KJV

Enter His gates with thanksgiving. And His courts with praise. Give thanks to Him; bless His name.

Psalm 100:4 KJV

Enter His gates with thanksgiving. And His courts with praise. Give thanks to Him; bless His name.

God, I could be so much more thankful! I am so ungrateful. I have so many times been so ungrateful. I was thinking about these gates which is wherever You are. That means that wherever I go, I am to be thankful. The gates are Your provision.

The courts: could that be when I am poised before Him? When I am in Your presence or and when I forget that I am in Your presence, I am to praise You. I get that.

Lord, I am working on being thankful. I am working on being more thankful. I am working on being more consistently thankful. I am working on being thankful and offering You thanks without being nudged and prompted. I know that whatever I am ungrateful for could be worse.

Lord, I bless You!

a former teenage girl

Psalm 100:5 KJV

For the Lord is good; His loving kindness is everlasting, and His faithfulness to all generations.

Psalm 100:5 KJV

For the Lord is good; His loving kindness is everlasting, and His faithfulness to all generations.

God, You are good but sometimes I do not act like it. I act like I do not know that You are a GOOD GOD. I hear it all the time. More importantly, I see it. The evidence of Your goodness is in my life. I need help living daily as if I know that goodness is real and for me.

God, I realized that Your loving kindness has existed since the beginning of my days. You love me. Your unconditional love fuels me and esteems me. Your unconditional love conditions me to receive the love of others. Your unconditional love conditions me to love You with the same loving kindness You teach. Your love will never expire.

God, You are faithful and it lasts always. To all of us? Lord, thank You for Your faithfulness toward us. Your ability to be faithful to me is truly risky because I know I am unworthy of Your faith. Thank You for having faith for me.

Psalm 23:3

He restores my soul; He guides me in the paths of righteousness for His

name's sake.

Psalm 23:3

He restores my soul; He guides me in the paths of righteousness for His name's sake.

God, You have given us many words, instructions and encouragement. Some of those words are anecdotes, some parables, and some songs. But this word says that You will restore my soul. Again that is over and over again—repeatedly. That restoration means that I won't be sad long or often. Restoration means that I won't be hurt long. Restoration suggests that I won't be angry long. Restoration means I can forgive. Restoration means I can love again. Thank You for constant, consistent restoration.

God, I always try to get off the path You created for righteousness. God remind me often, please, that the path is for me. Help me to remain on Your path. This is the best path.

Your name is the best name because Your name means so much and is so rich. I know I avoid You often. I know I ignore You because I want to be disobedient. Thank You for Your name.

a former teenage girl

Psalm 121:7 KJV

The Lord will protect you from all evil; He will keep your soul.

Psalm 121:7 KJV

The Lord will protect you from all evil; He will keep your soul.

All means all. God, Your protection is very important and valuable to me. God, You protect me from the evil one. Likewise, God, You protect me from the evil I do to myself. I could sabotage Your whole plan, but You do not let me! You keep me from hurting myself and others. You keep me from sacrificing the good that You have for me. Your keep me from keeping the good away from me. Thank You for keeping me from evil and the evil one.

Thank You for keeping my soul. Keeping me safe and whole is a huge job. I thank You for loving me. You keep my soul because You love me.

My soul is important to You and Your will for my life will prevail. Thank You for protecting me. I need it.

1 Corinthians 13:13 (MSG)

But for right now, until that completeness, we have three things to do to lead us toward that consummation: Trust steadily in God, hope unswervingly, love extravagantly. And the best of the three is love.

1 Corinthians 13:13 (MSG)

But for right now, until that completeness, we have three things to do to lead us toward that consummation: Trust steadily in God, hope unswervingly, love extravagantly. And the best of the three is love.

I know that I need help trusting steadily. I trust when it's convenient. I need to trust completely. God, You have given me enough to trust You for. You, created me and I should trust You just because You are God.

I thought unswervingly was self-made but I understand that it means that we need to hope with extreme focus. To let nothing change our courage of hope. Hope without fear. Regardless of the situation or hopelessness of the circumstances.

Love extravagantly?! Extravagant is defined as spending more than necessary, or wise, being wasteful, and exceeding the bounds of reason. Spending more love than necessary and wise. Love which exceeds the bounds of reason.

I want to do these things, especially love like that.

a former teenage girl

1 Corinthians 14:1 (MSG)

Go after a life of love as if your life depended on it—because it does. Give yourselves to the gifts God gives you.

1 Corinthians 14:1 (MSG)

Go after a life of love as if your life depended on it—because it does. Give yourselves to the gifts God gives you.

Lord when I consider the extravagant love You have for me and share, I become concerned. I get nervous because of my previous hurts and pains, I know that You are my healer, so I should love without reservation.

My life does depend on Love—how You love me and how I show and share that love with others. My life was built and developed on love. My love is formed from what I know. I love like I have learned love rather than love as a gift.

Love is a gift! Love is a gift worth sharing! It is the ultimate in what we share. When I consider how much love influences our lives, we must consider how our love motivates others. When I consider that I need to love for the rest of my life, I need to understand how I help others love.

Matthew 6:27

Who of you by worrying can add a single hour to his life?

Matthew 6:27

Who of you by worrying can add a single hour to his life?

I worry about some things. I worry about grades and friends and family. I worry about my future. I worry about the consequences of my sins. I worry about my academic choices. I worry about money for college. I do worry about what kind of adult I will become.

I wonder what kind of man I will marry. I wonder what my kids will be like. I wonder what type of mother I will be. I wonder what kind of grandmother I will be. I wonder what You will be in my life. I wonder what kind of cook I will be. I wonder what kind of career I will have.

I think about how much You love me. I count it all a blessing. I wonder if I will make You proud and disappoint all within the same short period of time. I consider my view of struggle and I know that I am not really struggling. I do thank You for the wisdom You share and the love You are manifest within me.

Matthew 6:33-34

[33] But seek first His kingdom and His righteousness, and all these thinks will be given to you as well. [34] Therefore do not worry about tomorrow, for tomorrow will worry about itself. Each day has enough trouble of its own.

Matthew 6:33-34

[33] But seek first His kingdom and His righteousness, and all these thinks will be given to you as well. [34] Therefore do not worry about tomorrow, for tomorrow will worry about itself. Each day has enough trouble of its own.

I know that You are the source of righteousness and seeking You first is the best thing from me. I am learning to hear Your voice and sense You in my spirit. I am learning to align myself with You and Your will and Your ways. You said that You would hear me when I pray.

I previously listed all of the things and aspects of my life that are on my mind and what I think matters to me right now. I think that I do think about a lot but I think about things that matter. I am not necessarily concerned about what I wear or how I look.

I try not to worry and just let things work out on their own. I just cannot stop considering how I factor into the inevitable equation of how this works out for me. I will do better to focus on You each day.

Matthew 7:7-8

⁷Ask and it will be given to you; seek and you will find; knock and the door will be opened to you. ⁸For everyone who asks receives; he who seeks finds; and to him who knocks, the door will be opened.

Matthew 7:7-8

[7]Ask and it will be given to you; seek and you will find; knock and the door will be opened to you. [8]For everyone who asks receives; he who seeks finds; and to him who knocks, the door will be opened.

Are You sure? Only within Your will. Not just because I want 'it.' I don't NEED everything I ask You for because it is not good for me. I at least know that. When I consider how this affects me, I am not sure exactly how I can apply this, however, I know that if seek You, I will find You. If I knock for You, the door will open to You. If I ask You, then I will receive.

I do believe that there needs to be wisdom in the asking. I cannot simply ask for just anything. And expect to receive it.

Seeking has many implications but it suggests that when I go after something I will find it. I need to make sure that Your Will is sought and I proceed.

Matthew 8:26

[Jesus] replied, "You of little faith, why are you so afraid?" Then he got up and rebuked the winds and waves, and it was completely calm.

Matthew 8:26

[Jesus] replied, "You of little faith, why are you so afraid?" Then he got up and rebuked the winds and waves, and it was completely calm.

You ask me this all the time: why am I afraid and what am I afraid of? I honestly do not know all of what I am afraid of. I don't know why I am afraid. I don't know when fear comes over me. I don't normally see my fear coming or feel it on the way.

You promised me that I would have faith based on Your love and development of me and my faith. Jesus, I know that You are able to execute Your plans because You are God.

If I trust You for Your strength and abilities, the disciples should not have been surprised by what You did and we should not be surprised at what You do for us daily. You keep Your word. Thank You for every promise You have ever kept.

Philippians 4:6

Be anxious for nothing, but in everything by prayer and supplication with thanksgiving let your requests be made known to God.

Philippians 4:6

Be anxious for nothing, but in everything by prayer and supplication with thanksgiving let your requests be made known to God.

I am not supposed to be anxious but sometimes I do. I get anxious about grades, parents, schools and boys. I get anxious about what my future holds. I am working to not be anxious for anything. It is really hard sometimes.

"By prayer" in everything make my requests by made known to You. I need to tell You what I want in prayer. "Supplication" in everything make my requests known to You. I need to tell You what I need in prayer. "With thanksgiving" make my requests be made known to You. I need to ask You for the answer to my anxieties in prayer. I need to do so with an humble spirit and a grateful heart and a pure motive.

You are the solution to my prayers, through prayer and supplication with thanksgiving.

a former teenage girl

Philippians 4:7

And the peace of God, which surpasses all comprehension, shall guard your hearts and your minds in Christ Jesus.

Philippians 4:7

And the peace of God, which surpasses all comprehension, shall guard your hearts and your minds in Christ Jesus.

Peace. I hear older people pray for peace all the time. Peace is a settling place where rest exists. Peace is a place where fear and anxiety cannot co-exist.

A peace which transcends all understanding because the existing conditions should contradict any possible peace. My situation is not so bad that I should not be peaceful so people can see Your peace and are confused that I am as well as I am.

Your peace will guard my heart and my mind against all things which prevent my peace. I am seeking Your peace. I need You to guard my heart and mind.

a former teenage girl

Philippians 4:13

I can do all things through Him who strengthens me.

Philippians 4:13

I can do all things through Him who strengthens me.

When I doubt, I try to remember I can do all things through You who strengthens me.

"I think that I can" was a phrase of character in a book titled, <u>The Little Engine that Could</u>. This train had a task of getting the freight to a location. The engine has not experience in this area but the desire was huge. The desire was the driving the force behind the chant.

I wonder if the engine knew the chant would go like this: "I think I can. I think I can do all things. I can do all things through Christ. I can do all things through Christ who strengthens me. I think I can. I think I can do all things. I can do all things through Christ. I can do all things through Christ who strengthens me. I think I can. I think I can do all things. I can do all things through Christ. I can do all things through Christ who strengthens me. I think I can. I think I can do all things. I can do all things through Christ. I can do all things through Christ who strengthens me."

I can do ALL things through Him who strengthens me.

a former teenage girl

Philippians 4:19

And my God shall supply all your needs according to His riches in glory in Christ Jesus.

Philippians 4:19

And my God shall supply all your needs according to His riches in glory in Christ Jesus.

God, I like the grammar in the Scripture. My God . . . your needs. As I share Christ with others, I like that I can say my God will supply your needs and be faithful to Your word. That's a powerful witness for me.

It's good news for me that God shall supply all my needs according to Your riches in glory in Christ Jesus. That is my comfort! You are indeed rich! I am glad that You share Your riches with me, even though I don't deserve it.

Thank You for supplying all of my needs! Thank You for Your provision!

Colossians 3:2

Set your mind on things above, not on the things that are on earth.

Colossians 3:2

Set your mind on things above, not on the things that are on earth.

So God, You don't want me to focus on earthly matters. Is that because that would distract me from You? It's likely that could happen. God, help me keep my complete focus on You.

I am not supposed to focus on my looks or my clothing. I am not supposed to focus on boys or makeup or hair. I am not supposed to concern myself with what others think of me.

Focus on YOU, GOD! And You alone. So I have to structure my life so that it is focused on what You want and what You command and what You desire and what You have planned and what You promise. Every day. Every hour of my life.

a former teenage girl

1 Thessalonians 5:15

See that no one repays another evil for evil, but always seek after that which is good for one another and for all man.

1 Thessalonians 5:15

See that no one repays another evil for evil, but always seek after that which is good for one another and for all man.

Revenge is relative to the conditions. We endure the wrath and meanness of each other. It seems that revenge seems natural but You say no, God. So how do I survive harm but not repay that person with my pain?

I am expected to "turn the other cheek," "be the bigger person," and, "forgive seventy times seven." It is hard. I am teased because I don't take revenge. I do think that I try to focus on You, God, so that I do not have to ask for forgiveness for revenge or the potential.

I am compassionate enough to do good for others even if they have wronged me. It is hard to do good with all others based on the safety issues we have. I am hoping that God, You are carefully eyeing those persons who come my way.

a former teenage girl

1 Thessalonians 5:18

In everything give thanks; for this is God's will for you in Christ Jesus.

1 Thessalonians 5:18

In everything give thanks; for this is God's will for you in Christ Jesus.

Give thanks. God, thank You for all that You are and all that You do and all that You created me to be. God, thank You for parents and families and friends. Thank You for the people who teach me and love me and respect me.

God, thank You for the teacher who makes me do my homework and take my education seriously. God, thank You for my church which loves me and teaches me and prays for me. God, thank You for the times when it feels like I am alone because that is when we are closest.

God, thank You for loving me and being my God. I know that I don't deserve to be loved by You all the time and I don't deserve to be forgiven by You but You do God. Thank You for being my God.

2 Timothy 2:22

Now flee from youthful lusts, and pursue righteousness, faith, love and peace, with those who call on the Lord from a pure heart.

2 Timothy 2:22

Now flee from youthful lusts, and pursue righteousness, faith, love and peace, with those who call on the Lord from a pure heart.

God, so this is a great time to share how hard this is. As I defined youthful lusts specifically for me, I am still working to understand myself.

Boys, sex, gossiping, bad behavior, mediocre grades—I am working on each of these characteristics within myself and what the influences are around me. Some times are tougher than others to choose righteousness.

I know that others, even adults, battle with this daily. I am depending on You, God, for the desire to pursue righteousness. God, help me pursue righteousness, faith, love and peace with a pure heart.

Hebrews 11:6

And without faith it is impossible to please Him, for he who can comes to God must believe that He is, and that He is a rewarder of those who seek Him.

Hebrews 11:6

And without faith it is impossible to please Him, for he who can comes to God must believe that He is, and that He is a rewarder of those who seek Him.

I can understand how You would be adamant about those of us who do not have faith in You all the time because we doubt when we get ready. I feel the same way when people do not believe in me. As a matter of fact, I do not speak, respect or trust people who did not believe or doubt me and speak negatively into my life.

Forgive me when I doubt. I am sure that I don't ask with as much faith at certain times. I do believe that You are God and God alone. I cannot believe in anything or anyone else.

God, the fact and knowledge of the fact that You will reward those of us who earnestly seek You is a great incentive to do exactly what You have asked. I will earnestly seek You even if I don't receive the exact reward I had in mind. Your rewards are great enough. They are elements I cannot give myself.

2 Timothy 1:5

For I am mindful of the sincere faith within you, which first dwelt in your grandmother Lois, and your mother Eunice, and I am sure that is in you as well.

2 Timothy 1:5

For I am mindful of the sincere faith within you, which first dwelt in your grandmother Lois, and your mother Eunice, and I am sure that is in you as well.

When Paul said this to Timothy, I considered if this could be said about me and my mother and grandmother. I know that I cannot do anything about their faith but I can be mindful of my own sincere measure of faith. This exhibit of faith should be evident. Additionally, if You have designed for me to be a mother and a grandmother, then I need to be prepared to share my faith at such a high level to leave a legacy of faith.

I am working daily to be more faithful. I do realize that faith is not cumulative or comprehensive because each event, situation, circumstance and today has the possibility to disrupt the faith I have. Some events could cause me to exhibit non—faith behavior.

Thank You for the many examples of faith which You give me so that when it gets tough, I have a resource to access so that I do not falter. Thank You, God.

a former teenage girl

2 Timothy 2:7

For God has not given us the spirit of timidity, but of power and love and discipline.

2 Timothy 2:7

For God has not given us the spirit of timidity, but of power and love and discipline.

I am scared because I had entered into new territory in my life. I know I am not supposed to be scared. I know You are not the author of fear. I do know that fear drives us apart. I move further away from You, God when I have fear in my heart.

God, only You can drive the spirit of fear from me.

God, You have given me power and love and discipline. The power to overcome fear and desire to escape fear. The love to share You with others. Discipline for the journey You have designed.

Thank You for Your thoughtfulness!

a former teenage girl

Psalm 119:11

I have hidden your word in my heart that I might not sin against you.

Psalm 119:11

I have hidden your word in my heart that I might not sin against you.

What I learn I know forever. What is not truly a part of me would disappear shortly. At least that is true in science class or in my foreign language class.

God, Your word should be a huge, intense and deeply rooted within me. If the words of Your Word are interwoven into my soul, then I will have internal accountability. God, Your words will speak to me when sin is presented.

If it is hidden within my heart, it is not exposed to others but represents the behavior and speech which I share and show. Thank You God for Your word and its ultimate guidance.

Jeremiah 1:5

Before I formed you in the womb I knew you, before you were born I set you

apart, I appointed you as a prophet to the nations.

Jeremiah 1:5

Before I formed you in the womb I knew you, before you were born I set you apart, I appointed you as a prophet to the nations.

God, You are the author of my life. Some of my friends think that they are "mistakes" because their parents were not married or they have much older or younger siblings. But this Word contradicts all that they think and everything that they have been told or assume.

This Word says that we are all intentional. We need to behave like it.

You set me apart—even from Your other creations? I am uniquely different and authentically designed. You created me for specific activities and creative ventures.

You have assigned me to bring clarity to nations. I will work to know Your voice and to whom to speak.

a former teenage girl

Psalm 19:14

May these words of my mouth and this meditation of my heart be pleasing in
Your sight, Lord, my Rock and my Redeemer.

Psalm 19:14

May these words of my mouth and the meditation of my heart be pleasing in Your sight, Lord, my Rock and my Redeemer.

Lord, may the words which come out of my mouth and the meditations of my heart be pleasing in Your sight! Lord, are the words I use pleasing in Your sight? Sometimes the words are not pleasing. I know this because I usually regret them immediately.

Lord, thank You for not punishing me according to the death I bring with my tongue. I know that with all the gifts I have from You within, I know that You intend for people who are in my path to be blessed by me; not to be condemned by me.

Lord, return my heart to an upright, clean position. Is there a way that my heart can ever please You? I want please You even though it is easier to do wrong than avoid sin.

a former teenage girl

Revelation 3:16

So, because you are lukewarm—neither hot nor cold—I am about to spit you out of My mouth.

Revelation 3:16

So, because you are lukewarm—neither hot nor cold—I am about to spit you out of My mouth.

This is the one thing that irritates me the most: lukewarm people. It means that they are indecisive. Indecisive people cannot be trusted. God, thank You for ensuring that I am not lukewarm.

God, I love You and thank You for being transparent with us about Your expectations and preferences. I know that being lukewarm is of an indecisive spirit.

I am concerned about lukewarm people because they can and will change often. They will sell themselves and others out in order to gain for personal reasons.

Lukewarm people: pick a temperature.

a former teenage girl

Proverbs 23:7 (KJV)

For as he thinketh in his heart, so is he.

Proverbs 23:7 (KJV)

For as he thinketh in his heart, so is he.

So what I think is what is in my heart. So what is in my heart I take action on?

I am what is inside me. The change only comes from You working on my inside to the outside. The good within my heart is what shines on the outside.

This is telling me what I have to protect my heart from unwholesome influences so that they won't change me for the worse.

God please perfect what is in my heart.

Matthew 11:28

Come to me, all you who are weary and heavy ladened. And I will give your

rest.

Matthew 11:28

Come to me, all you who are weary and heavy ladened. And I will give your rest.

Thanks for inviting me to You, God. Thank You for inviting me to come to You. Without strings. Without conditions. Without judgment. Without vanity.

Thank You for calling me because I am tired, weary and worn. Thank You for supporting me when I am heavily burdened. Thank You for accepting me and my burdens, regardless of how they became my burdens.

Lord, how are You defining rest? How do I know that I can put the full weight of who I am and who I am not on You? Because You said so. This will take practice because I do not give away my burdens because my disappointment was so widespread that I vowed to never do it again.

Thank You for providing me rest—complete and comprehensive rest. A safe place for my needs, issues and struggles.

a former teenage girl

Luke 23:34

Jesus said, "Father, forgive them, for they do not know what they are doing."

Luke 23:34

Jesus said, "Father, forgive them, for they do not know what they are doing."

Thank You for defending me. Jesus, You ask God to forgive me. The ultimate definition in protection. The protection You provide is above any that others could attempt to provide.

Jesus, Your unselfishness again sets the standard. You put me before Yourself again. Jesus for having the wisdom that I need to function daily, thank You.

God, I do NOT know! I do NOT know what I am doing! With ANYTHING! I lie. I hurt others. I take You for granted. I miss the details of Your love. Daily! I know this based on how they crucified You, Jesus, but the actions were sinning against You. We continue to sin against You daily so thank You for hearing my cry and answering my plea.

And, AGAIN giving me what I do NOT deserve!

Romans 8:26

In the same way, the Spirit helps us in our weakness. We do not know what we ought to pray for, but the Spirit himself intercedes for us with groans that words cannot express.

Romans 8:26

In the same way, the Spirit helps us in our weakness. We do not know what we ought to pray for, but the Spirit himself intercedes for us with groans that words cannot express.

Jesus, thank You for the gift of the Holy Spirit! The Holy Spirit is for me. I know that You sent Jesus and the Holy Spirit to save me and lead me and share with me what You want me to know.

God, thank You for knowing my weaknesses, acknowledging them and offering me a Helper for those weaknesses. Lord, the Holy Spirit is so wonderful to me and for me. The Holy Spirit helps me pray. The Holy Spirit helps me listen.

The Holy Spirit intercedes for me when I don't know what to say to You. The Holy Spirit helps me share with You the stuff I am afraid to tell You because I am afraid of what You are going to say because I already know that I have disappointed You.

God, thank You for the Holy Spirit—my intercessor.

1 Corinthians 10:13

No temptation has seized you except what is common to man. And God is faithful; he will not let you be tempted beyond what you can bear. But when you are tempted, he will also provide a way out so you can stand up under it.

1 Corinthians 10:13

No temptation has seized you except what is common to man. And God is faithful; he will not let you be tempted beyond what you can bear. But when you are tempted, he will also provide a way out so you can stand up under it.

God, there is so much temptation around me. I could date anyone or have sex with anyone. I have the option of drugs and alcohol and other distractions that I don't even know. Lord, thank You for keeping me strong when temptation comes my way.

God, daily there are new stories about young people around me who are on drugs, are pregnant, and are dropping out of school. They are failing in school. They are stealing and joining gangs. They need to feel Your love like I know it.

Thank You for the power and accessibility of Your love. Thank You for the investment of Your strength.

a former teenage girl

Ephesians 4:32

Be kind and compassionate to one another, forgiving each other, just as in Christ God forgave you.

Ephesians 4:32

Be kind and compassionate to one another, forgiving each other, just as in Christ God forgave you.

God, I am kind to others but it is not always easy. Help me get past my desire to get people back for being unkind to me. God, I want to be kind all the time. It is hard sometimes. Thank You for providing me more opportunities to be kind.

God, I did not learn compassion until I needed some compassion for my situations. I am compassionate because I know how it feels to need that compassion. I know that others have the same compassion. I know that my compassion could potentially encourage someone to live.

God, I am still working on timely forgiveness. You forgive me. I forgive me. I forgive others. Thank You for loving me enough.

Jude 24

Now onto him that is able to keep you from falling, and to present you

faultless before the presence of his glory with exceeding joy.

Jude 24

Now onto him that is able to keep you from falling, and to present you faultless before the presence of his glory with exceeding joy.

God, I owe You honor because You keep me from falling. I can cause myself to stumble. You save me from myself. Everyday!

God, how awesome are You to present me faultless before Yourself. When You know what I have done and ALL that You have forgiven me for and You still forgive me and completely cleanse me from the wrath I deserve.

Thank You for being You and caring for me in this manner.

a former teenage girl

Colossians 3:23

Whatever you do, work at it with all your heart, as working for the Lord, not for men.

Colossians 3:23

Whatever you do, work at it with all your heart, as working for the Lord, not for men.

God, You are the author of my work ethic. I am being trained to give what I put my hands on my very best work ethic—no excuses. You expect my best on EVERYTHING! I am adjusting to give my best even when I do not like the project or person or concept.

I know I do some things better than others because I like some things better. What I did not know was that I owe my work ethic and my talents to You, God.

I am to share my gifts with those in my reach because it will bring You glory. Thank You for reminding me of where my work ethic was designed and perfected.

a former teenage girl

Ephesians 3:17

So that Christ may dwell in your hearts through faith; and that you, being

rooted and grounded in love.

Ephesians 3:17

So that Christ may dwell in your hearts through faith; and that you, being rooted and grounded in love.

Christ dwells within my heart! That is the only way I can live is that You live within me. My heart is alive because of Your indwelling. My heart is lifted because it is supported by You, O God.

Christ is showing me faith. God strengthens my faith in such a way that I almost miss the transition. There were events which have built and molded my faith. These experiences have been so rich that only now looking back can I recognize Your hand, God.

Lord, love is an emotion that I cannot afford to live without. Lord, I know that I have an interesting definition and how it was formed. Love, You rooted and grounded me in love. What I know is that You started my life with love and daily You remind me of Your love is my basis for all things. You are my definition of love.

Colossians 3:8

But now you must rid yourself of all such things as these: anger, rage,

malice, slander, and filthy language from your lips.

Colossians 3:8

But now you must rid yourself of all such things as these: anger, rage, malice, slander, and filthy language from your lips.

God, the "cool thing" in high school is filthy language.

Slander is gossip right? Slander means that I say things that may not be true about others as well as share bad things which are true about others with others. Help me with renewing myself from slander and gossip in other words which have the potential to hurt the subject of the dialogue.

God, I ask You to control my attitude, actions and behavior. I need You to protect my mouth so that I do not hurt others with my anger, rage, malice, slander and filthy language. My lips communicate what is on my mind and in my heart. If I am not angry, I cannot express anger. If I have not been harmed, then I cannot express rage. If I have not been endangered, that I cannot show malice. If I have not found laughter in someone else's misfortune, then I would not delight in slander. If I did not have heard in my heart, then I would not happy with the language.

Lord remind me that You offer enough grace to remove the temptation to respond to others in this manner regardless of what has happened to me.

a former teenage girl

Colossians 3:10

And have put on the new self, which is being renewed in the image of the

Creator.

Colossians 3:10

And have put on the new self, which is being renewed in the image of the Creator.

Lord, what is a new self? What do I shed to become new? Is my new self nicer? Is my new self calmer? Is my new self a better student? Is my new self by better prayer? Is my new self better at relationships? Is my new self better at time management?

What does my new self look like? How does my new self look? Who can help me with my new self?

This alignment with God is unique. I did not realize how far away I was from the original image of me—what God designed.

I am a work in progress. God is showing me ways to be new in Christ. He is showing me daily.

Genesis 50:15

When Joseph's brothers saw that the father was dead, they said, "What if Joseph should bear a grudge against us and pay us back in full for all the wrong which we did to him!"

Genesis 50:15

When Joseph's brothers saw that the father was dead, they said, "What if Joseph should bear a grudge against us and pay us back in full for all the wrong which we did to him!"

Joseph was an example of what to do. His brothers were an example of what not to do. His brothers are afraid of what Joseph would do to them because of what they did to him. Joseph saved his brothers.

God, You are amazing. Joseph story tells me that when we pray thanking God for keeping us from things seen and unseen we have no idea of which we speak. What appeared horrible turned out to be GREAT for Joseph. So great that his brothers benefited from it as well.

Work through me God so that I avoid revenge. It is hard to avoid sometimes. Help me reach that level where I can please You. Thank You for giving me an example to follow and to refer to when it gets really difficult to walk away from the desire to take revenge. Thank You for providing me an escape when I want to be vengeful against someone who has wronged me.

Ephesians 3:20 KJV

Now unto Him who is able to do exceeding abundantly above all that we ask or think, according to the power that worketh in us.

Ephesians 3:20 KJV

Now unto Him who is able to do exceeding abundantly above all that we ask or think, according to the power that worketh in us.

So I have power within me? Where did I get that power from? How do I access that power? I want to use the power You have given me. Then what did You want me to use that power for?

Lord, I want and need a lot from You. Mostly Your direction and guidance. Please know that without Your guidance, life is simply not complete. I know that You supply my needs and wants through those You put around me. I think that sometimes I disappoint You because I don't act like it. I love You. I want to please You and I want to properly access that power You have given me.

Lord, thank You for not letting the devil use me when he chooses. Thank You for letting me walk away from temptation. I know that's what I ask or think is minimal. I consider it a privilege to have what I do have—the gifts You have given me.

Ephesians 6:18

And pray in the Spirit on all occasions with all kinds of prayers and requests. With this in mind, be alert and always keep praying for all the saints.

Ephesians 6:18

And pray in the Spirit on all occasions with all kinds of prayers and requests. With this in mind, be alert and always keep praying for all the saints.

Lord, teach me how to pray better! Lord, I want to talk to You more consistently and more reverently. Lord, I want to learn how to pray for others. I know that prayer is powerful. I know that I grow closer to You through prayer. I do want to grow closer to You.

Somebody petitions You on my behalf? I know that someone prays for me but what do they say when they pray? What do I pray for when I pray for others? I want to petition Your will and Your desire.

Perseverance requires focus. Lord, help me focus and persevere through what You share with me and who You have planned for me to become. Keep me alert, Lord. Help me maintain my focus.

a former teenage girl

Ephesians 5:1-2

Therefore be imitators of God, as beloved children; and walk in love, just as Christ also loved you, and gave Himself up for us, an offering and a sacrifice to God as a fragrant aroma.

Ephesians 5:1-2

Therefore be imitators of God, as beloved children; and walk in love, just as Christ also loved you, and gave Himself up for us, an offering and a sacrifice to God as a fragrant aroma.

Lord, it is hard to imitate You. You are so perfect. I am so imperfect. I know that it is not how it was supposed to be. I am trying to be better every day. Thank You for loving me. I am trying to walk in love. Sometimes love is hard to see or hear or know. Thank You for loving me so that I have a real definition.

I cry often when I consider what Jesus did for me. Jesus did it for me. He defined love for me in such a tangible way. I cannot think of who I would die for so dying for people I do not know would be virtually impossible.

God, You experienced the greatest sacrifice—Your Son. Thank You for being God—the One who loves me even when I disappoint.

a former teenage girl

1 John 4:19

We love, because He first loved us.

1 John 4:19

We love, because He first loved us.

You want us to love like You do? God, You know love is hard. I am trying to love You like You love me, so loving others is a big challenge. I am working on loving You through my school work and cleaning my room and not talking back to my parents. I am working on loving You when I respect my mother and father and family.

I am trying to love You like I am supposed to through everything in my life. I am working to love others like You designed. I think other people selectively deserve my love. I know You don't condone that. I am working to love others but because of what they do or don't do, I have not loved them.

Thank You for loving me unconditionally. I really think pride and not wanting to be taken advantage of stops us from loving unconditionally. Work on my heart Lord so that I can give authentic love.

1 John 4:18

There is no fear in love; but perfect love casts out of fear, because fear involves punishment. The one who fears is not perfected in love.

1 John 4:18

There is no fear in love; but perfect love casts out of fear, because fear involves punishment. The one who fears is not perfected in love.

Fear and love cannot exist within the same person; in the same mind; in the same heart; in the same spirit.

Perfect love? Perfect love. Perfect love! God, Only Yours is perfect. Only Yours can be perfect. No other love is perfect. Not even mine. I am working on the unconditional love which is perfect according to Your definition and Your example. Your love comforts and drives out fear, which was brought on by my lack of knowledge and experience, lack of faith and trust.

When I believe and know and trust is that You love me then I would not have to be fearful. If I understand Your love for me, I do not have to be fearful so I can avoid punishment, which I normally self-impose. God, Thank You for Your perfect love.

1 John 5:4

For whatever is born of God overcomes the world; and this is the victory

that holds overcome the world our faith.

1 John 5:4

For whatever is born of God overcomes the world; and this is the victory that holds overcome the world our faith.

I am born out of You, God.

Because I am born out of God, I can overcome the world.

Our faith is the victory of overcoming the world.

You created, birthed and destined me. When I consider what I am up against, I am reminded that You have provided me with faith to overcome my challenges. I need to access that faith—faith that helps me remember that You are in charge of my every step and my every move.

God, You have encouraged me with victory. Lord, sometimes I do not thank You enough for those are victories. Thank You for affirming my faith.

3 John 2

Beloved, I pray that in all aspects you may prosper and be in good health, just as your soul prospers.

3 John 2

Beloved, I pray that in all aspects you may prosper and be in good health, just as your soul prospers.

Lord,

I commit my health to You, God. I commit to make every effort to keep the body we occupy together as healthy as possible. Lord, keep me from the temptation of each and every drug and alcohol and overeating. Help me avoid any substance which will alter my body in a negative manner.

I commit my prosperity to You and the work You have called me to do. Lord, I seek You and all of my endeavors as I want to be in your will. Thank You for my prosperity, not just financial wealth but also a spiritual, emotional and physical wealth. I seek to crave You. I pray to please You and follow Your will, aligning myself to You daily.

My Lord, feed my soul with Your word, will and knowledge of the Holy Spirit so that my soul can prosper for You.

Lord, thank You for prospering me and love, gifts and deeds. I can certainly appreciate this relationship.

Galatians 5:22-23

But the fruit of the Spirit is love, joy, peace, patience, kindness, goodness, faithfulness, gentleness, self-control; against such things there is no law.

Galatians 5:22-23

But the fruit of the Spirit is love, joy, peace, patience, kindness, goodness, faithfulness, gentleness, self-control; against such things there is no law.

So I can have love, joy, peace, patience, kindness, goodness, faithfulness, gentleness, and self-control with no consequence. The challenge is gaining access to all those things. At the same time.

I can do some of them some of the time but not all of them at the same time. The ones which are hardest are self-control, goodness, kindness, and love.

I am working on the total investment and engagement of all of the fruit. Lord, help me with those areas. I would be better person if I do so. I need to be a better expression of all who You are.

a former teenage girl

Galatians 5:22-23

But the fruit of the Spirit is love.

Galatians 5:22-23

But the fruit of the Spirit is love.

Fruit is postured as a singular noun, but there are nine elements. How is that grammatically correct?

My love is so conditional based on how I feel and what others feel about me based on activities and behavior.

Joy is an expression of fullness regarding how You fill us.

Peace is the resting of my heart and soul.

Patience is a virtue and an art based on God's provision.

Kindness is my ability to be kind to ALL persons at all time.

Goodness is my ability to be good to myself and others.

Faithfulness is my obedience to God and His plan.

Gentleness is my ability to handle others well in regards to emotional, spiritual, and physical compassion.

Self-control is my ability to say no when I should, control my tone and my words and behave in a pleasing manner.

God, I have a lot of work to do.

a former teenage girl

1 Corinthians 16:14

Let all that you do be done in love.

1 Corinthians 16:14

Let all that you do be done in love.

God, the total sum of who You are is love. The total expectation of us that You have is to love others and do what we do in love. I am trying to do activities and access to others in love. Love is a verb. So I need to be love.

Me as a verb of love. I am love! If I say it over and over again then I can be love. Real love. It is an amazing concept—to be love. I want to be love. Again I am often concerned how others will treat me if I am too "soft." I am not able to understand the concept of total love because I have been wronged.

So as I do all that I do in love, I have some work to do. I am working on being love, doing it in love and understanding how to express the love You define.

a former teenage girl

Galatians 5:19

Now the deeds of the flesh are evident: which are immorality, sensuality

Galatians 5:19

Now the deeds of the flesh are evident: which are immorality, sensuality

Lord, I cannot hide my sins from You. Sometimes that is hard for me. I want to sin without consequence.

I had to look up those words: immorality, impurity and sensuality. Immorality is defined as not conforming to the patterns of conduct usually excepted or established as consistent with principles of personal and social ethics. Impurity is not morally pure or proper. Sensuality is the preoccupation with the gratification of the senses or appetites; carnal; worldly.

So I stand in need of correction in these areas. So many of my friends resort to this behavior because we want the attention of boys. Because we think that they make us feel better about ourselves, we do things that we think they will like. We are so short of acceptance in other areas including our parents and some of our friends.

Help me avoid these areas. So many of us have done things we hope our mothers never find out. Lord, forgive us. Help us to reach for You to avoid the flesh—ours and others.

a former teenage girl

Galatians 5:20

idolatry, sorcery, enmities, strife, jealousy, outbursts of anger, disputes,

dissensions, factions

Galatians 5:20

idolatry, sorcery, enmities, strife, jealousy, outbursts of anger, disputes, dissensions, factions

God, so these are more words I looked up. So idolatry is my love for clothes, music, food and television. These activities come before You. Sorcery is witchcraft which I do not have any connection with. Strife is creating conflict between others because of poor intentions of my own. Jealousy is when someone wants what belongs to others. Normally, one person is driven to jealousy because we make the wrong thing important.

Outbursts of anger is when I act based on emotion and without control. I could easily take a moment before reacting or responding. Sometimes we do things to others intentionally to make them angry. Disputes are arguments or debates, quarreling for the sake of being disagreeable. Dissension is more discord. Factions are cliques, which we live and thrive on.

None of these are good. They only further separate us from You, Your purpose and people we should love. Lord, help me distance myself from those who take such actions. Further, Lord, help me be a better leader who takes a stand for right even when it is someone who I think is my friend.

Galatians 5:21

envying, drunkenness, carousing, and things like these, of which I forewarn you just as I have forewarn you that those who practice such things shall not inherit the kingdom of God.

Galatians 5:21

envying, drunkenness, carousing, and things like these, of which I forewarn you just as I have forewarn you that those who practice such things shall not inherit the kingdom of God.

So I am not to envy or be drunk, drinking excessively and frequently. These things along with the other things will keep me from inheriting the kingdom of God.

That is not my desire. I want Your love and to inherit the fullness of Your wealth, which is the kingdom of God. Help me. Steer me away from these traps.

In Jesus' name!

a former teenage girl

James 1:2

Consider it pure joy, my brothers, whenever you face trials of many kinds.

James 1:2

Consider it pure joy, my brothers, whenever you face trials of many kinds.

When I hear other Christians say this, I am in awe. My attitude does not speak to this well. I asked someone and she said that when trials come is because You trust us to make it through. That You are testing us so that we know what we are made of—what we can actually accomplish when we place our faith, trust in God and with total surrender.

So he said that we should be joyful because You are investing in us and You are proving to us who You are through our trials. If You could not trust us to pass, You would not test us. You test and try those You trust.

Thank You for trusting me enough to try, knowing that I would not quit or fall short of Your expectations. Thank You for proving to me what You already know about me, but You need me to understand.

a former teenage girl!

James 1:3

because you know that the testing of your faith develops perseverance

James 1:3

because you know that the testing of your faith develops perseverance

God! You are going to continue to test my faith in ways that I cannot imagine. Clearly, I am going to go through some things. You are showing me how faithful You are.

Perseverance is the steady persistence in a course of action, a purpose, especially in spite of difficulties, obstacles or discouragement. Perseverance needs to be developed over time so that You will be proven. I will see this developed over time in my life and in various areas so that I can be a complete work.

My faith will be developed as well so that I can stand through the tough times. I respect Christians who lived through the issues I need to know that I can do the same.

I know that You are there so I am ready.

James 1:4

Perseverance must finish its perfect work so that you may be mature and complete, not lacking anything.

James 1:4

Perseverance must finish its perfect work so that you may be mature and complete, not lacking anything.

So as I said perseverance is going to need to keep happening for the different levels we each need to reach.

God, my question is do the tests ever end on this side of heaven? It does not matter though. I want to be complete. I like to finish what I start. I am focused on finish. I do not like to lose. I do not lose well. I do not quit. I am a finisher. I want to be complete.

God, You complete me. Only You can!

Maturity is always the goal. I consider maturity necessary and not easily attained. We are not wise about all things so that there is still a need for You. So that we will seek You consistently.

God, You are growing and shaping my perseverance to perfection. I know that in order to grow and develop that means that I have to be close to You. I never want to be out of Your reach.

James 1:5

If any of you lacks wisdom, he should ask God, who gives generously and to all without finding fault, and it will be given to him.

James 1:5

If any of you lacks wisdom, he should ask God, who gives generously and to all without finding fault, and it will be given to him.

Wisdom, God? The knowledge of what is true or right coupled with just judgment as to action. So knowledge coupled with good judgment means that decisions I make should be based on these elements. There are areas where I am certainly ignorant but in time, wisdom will be abound within me.

In the meantime, I'll continue to ask for wisdom and seek your face for the wisdom I need each day.

Solomon was wise because You blessed him. Jesus was wise because He is Your son. I want to be wise because I am Your child. People respect wise people and You love wise people so I can be a representative of You by following Your wisdom.

Thank You for giving wisdom freely.

a former teenage girl

James 1:12

Blessed is the man who perseveres under trial, because when he has stood the test, he will receive the crown of life that God has promised to those who love Him.

James 1:12

Blessed is the man who perseveres under trial, because when he has stood the test, he will receive the crown of life that God has promised to those who love Him.

God, more reason to persevere. I do want Your blessings. I want Your blessings because You have them set aside for me. Your blessings are not based on conditions nor withdrawn from me based on any other superficial means.

I want to stand the test! I so want to complete Your perfect work! I really want to do the work You have for me to do. I certainly want to pass ALL of Your tests. I know that I won't pass all the tests but I want to try to pass them all.

You promised me the crown of life if I stood Your tests and persevered my storms. I do love You. I want that crown. I am in need of Your help to earn it.

James 3:8-9

[8] *but no man can tame the tongue. It is a restless evil, full of deadly poison.* [9] *With the tongue we praise our Lord and father, and with it we can curse men, who have been made in God's likeness.*

James 3:8-9

[8] *but no man can tame the tongue. It is a restless evil, full of deadly poison.* [9] *With the tongue we praise our Lord and father, and with it we can curse men, who have been made in God's likeness.*

Lord, wow! When I consider what comes from my mouth, I am ashamed. I gossip. I am negative about others. I am sometimes mean to others. I do not allow people around me that are not cool or have the same social status that I have. I use my tongue to make others feel worse. I use it to make myself look better. Better than what I really am.

I am going to be better about treating others better. I am convicted about how I speak of others. I would not want to be talked about like in such a manner. My self-esteem may wilt if I heard those same things about myself or was on the margin of the crowd.

God, help me be an advocate for all people around me. Let me be a change agent for my age group. Let me keep Your commands and promises close to my heart and mind so that obedience is not so hard. Help me reduce bullying with the influence You have gifted me with.

Control my tongue so that my mouth will be aligned to Your likeness.

James 3:10

Out of the same mouth come praise and cursing. My brothers, this should

not be.

James 3:10

Out of the same mouth come praise and cursing. My brothers, this should not be.

Lord God, <u>please</u> forgive me! This is true! I have praised You and cursed others with the same mouth, mind and heart! I should be cursed. Yet You forgive! Every time! You have allowed me to continue my life in spite of my malice.

Lord, forgive me! Help me control my tongue each day, minute by minute. Remind me to find something constructive to say rather than the horrible insults I have gathered to use against that person.

Father, thank You for showing me the error in my ways. I am working daily to be more positive, abandoning death by pain. Some of what I have said is not worthy of repeating and certainly do not want them ever to say it to me. Thank You God for Your grace!

James 4:2

You want something but don't get it. You kill and covet, but you cannot have what you want. You quarrel and fight. You do not have, because you do not ask God.

James 4:2

You want something but don't get it. You kill and covet, but you cannot have what you want. You quarrel and fight. You do not have, because you do not ask God.

"By any means necessary" was a phrase which was birthed during a civil rights movement by Malcolm X. This phrase can be used by how we pursue material possessions and other things we want.

God, You grant me the needs and wants as You see fit. If I don't ask, then I won't receive.

I know that it is not good to steal, kill, covet, quarrel, fight and destroy what belongs to others. I will ask You for my needs and desires. And I will WAIT for Your response.

a former teenage girl

Ephesians 2:8-9

[8] *For it is by grace you have been saved, through faith—and this is not from yourselves, it is the gift of God—*[9] *not by works, so that no one can boast.*

Ephesians 2:8-9

[8] For it is by grace you have been saved, through faith—and this is not from yourselves, it is the gift of God—[9] not by works, so that no one can boast.

God! You SAVED ME! BY GRACE! You saved me because You wanted me saved. Because You wanted to. I am learning faith as a teenager. It is not easy because faith seems so vague. As I hear more and learn more about faith, I keep looking for areas of my life what I can actively exercise my faith and share it with others.

For now, my faith has been shaped by believing that if I study hard so that when I sit for the exam that the information will come to my remembrance and that I would not be anxious about the results. My faith is being formed. I am sure that there will be other events designed to test my faith. I am not necessarily looking forward to those events but I know that You are there.

I thank You for Your gift of salvation! Thank You for the fairness of Your salvation. You really know us. If we had to compete for Your salvation or grace or Your love, that could be dangerous and we would not share the good news about You.

Ephesians 2:10

For we are God's workmanship, created in Christ Jesus to do good works,

which God prepared in advance for us to do.

Ephesians 2:10

For we are God's workmanship, created in Christ Jesus to do good works, which God prepared in advance for us to do.

I am ecstatic that God created me! I know that You made me exactly how You wanted me. I don't always thank You for creating me. Sometimes I even complain about the workmanship. Too short. Too tall. Too dark. Too light. Too tall. Too heavy. Too thin. But then You remind me that You are the author of ALL things. You are intentional with my details.

You created me. Because You created me, You created work for me to do. Good work to do. I have to be watchful of the opportunity to do good work. My good work starts with my grades in school and pursuing the gifts You have given me.

God, You already planned my work. I think that I will be presented this work in such a manner that I will know that work is Your plan for me. Lord, keep my eyes and hands sharp for the tasks.

a former teenage girl

Ephesians 6:23

For the wages of sin is death, but the gift of God is eternal life in Christ

Jesus our Lord.

Ephesians 6:23

For the wages of sin is death, but the gift of God is eternal life in Christ Jesus our Lord.

Because of my sins, I am supposed to be dead. That is quite sobering. The gift of Your Son and His death, burial and resurrection changed all of that. Those significant events change my destiny. We talk about this at church all the time.

Thank You for eternal life! You could've done so much differently! You could have changed Your mind! Thank You for planning my life so that I could spend the rest of it with You!

I know there is no way to repay You. Thank You for saving me!

Romans 10:9-10

⁹ That if you confess with your mouth, "Jesus is Lord," and believe in your heart that God raised Him from the dead, you will be saved. ¹⁰ For it is with your heart that you believe and are justified, and it is with your mouth that you confess and are saved.

Romans 10:9-10

[9] That if you confess with your mouth, "Jesus is Lord," and believe in your heart that God raised Him from the dead, you will be saved. [10] For it is with your heart that you believe and are justified, and it is with your mouth that you confess and are saved.

I think You have outlined how to be saved fairly well but not everyone understands. Does their lack of salvation break Your heart? As God, how long do You let them follow the wrong path? I am glad that didn't happen to me.

I said Jesus is Lord and I believe in my heart that You are real and have died for my sins. My confession saved me. My heart is powerful and worthwhile for persuading us to take action.

It is true Your power exists within us. It is true You put it there. The power of my tongue is underrated. It has much more power than I know.

a former teenage girl

Romans 5:8-9

⁸ But God demonstrates His own love for us in this: while we were still sinners, Christ died for us. ⁹ Since we have now been justified by His blood, how much more shall we be saved from God's wrath through Him!

Romans 5:8-9

[8] But God demonstrates His own love for us in this: while we were still sinners, Christ died for us. [9] Since we have now been justified by His blood, how much more shall we be saved from God's wrath through Him!

You demonstrated Your love for us. You do it over and over again. I do not always demonstrate my love for You. Certainly not through my actions and deeds, my words or behavior, respect or lack thereof.

Christ died with full knowledge that we would continue to sin. Who does that? Only Jesus! Otherwise no one does that. We stop being friends, distance family and abandon all others when they hurt us and repeatedly so. But not You, oh God. You love us, forgive us, and redeem us DAILY in the only way You can and You were the only One who would.

You are the only person who will redeem others through Yourself. It is a hard concept to accept, because we do not know and are not willing to follow Your example. You chose forgiveness over wrath as long as my behavior warrants such.

a former teenage girl

2 Corinthians 12:7

To keep me from becoming conceited because of these surpassingly great revelations, there was given me a thorn in my flesh, a messenger of Satan, to torment me.

2 Corinthians 12:7

To keep me from becoming conceited because of these surpassingly great revelations, there was given me a thorn in my flesh, a messenger of Satan, to torment me.

The thorn is quite a measure. I am conceited sometimes. I believe I am beautiful and talented and I can have "the big head." God, I know that You do not like my conceit.

My thorns are an occasional bad grade, an occasional bad clothing or/and bad hair day, and sometimes my relationships. Paul had a different thorn. The thorn is to remind us to remember You, God.

I need direction from You. Help me sharpen my ears, heart and mind to hear Your voice and Your words delivered by others. Thank You for this much attention.

a former teenage girl

2 Corinthians 12:8

Three times I pleaded with the Lord to take it away from me.

2 Corinthians 12:8

Three times I pleaded with the Lord to take it away from me.

God, I begged You for relief from the weight of my family. God, You said no. You said that You would walk with me, that You would care for me as I am enduring their harm, malice, disgust, hurt, and danger. They seek to break me yet You, God, do not allow the total of their intentions to become true. God, You love me in spite of their intense hate.

I begged You God to relieve me of the pressure of my studies and work. You again said no. You whispered to me that my work requires my attention, my intense, intentional attention. God, thank You for helping me focus and memorize and learn and succeed with work and studies. Thank You for giving me what I need to keep me moving toward the mark of academic excellence.

I begged You Lord to relieve me from relationships which will hurt me. God, You said You would heal me from my hurt and help me recover when I am harmed.

You then said that all of these events and persons and activities will help me grow.

2 Corinthians 12:9

But he said to me, "My grace is sufficient for you, for my power is made perfect in weakness." Therefore I will boast all the more gladly about my weaknesses, so that Christ's power may rest on me.

2 Corinthians 12:9

But he said to me, "My grace is sufficient for you, for my power is made perfect in weakness." Therefore I will boast all the more gladly about my weaknesses, so that Christ's power may rest on me.

My weakness is not easy either. Just keep me close to You, God because I need You. I need your grace, whether I know when You actually give it or not. The fact that I know it's being given is the greatest thing.

God, You are saying that You are more powerful when I am weak. When I am weak, that is when I depend fully on You and share with others how You bless me in spite of my weaknesses and issues, which are usually perceived.

When I am "strong," then I "forget" I am still weak and I become proud and boast. You remind me that You are God in my weaknesses. You and Your grace are sufficient! You are enough. Thank You for reminding me.

2 Corinthians 12:10

That is why for Christ sake, I delight in weaknesses, in insults, in hardships, in persecutions, in difficulties. For when I am weak, then I am strong.

2 Corinthians 12:10

That is why for Christ sake, I delight in weaknesses, in insults, in hardships, in persecutions, in difficulties. For when I am weak, then I am strong.

Paul is in a place I am working to be. . . 'I delight in weakness.' I am not quite there but I do understand that You are closer when I acknowledge and submit to my weaknesses.

Paul delights in weaknesses, insults, hard ships, persecutions and difficulties. I will be growing to that level. I do not need to be convinced. I will be reminded. It is a reminder of You. A dedication and commitment to You.

Paul refers to a strength that only You can provide and support. The strength You provide Israel. Not that 'strength' that storms can crush or blow away. Paul is truthful and this is a BIG lesson for all of us. We need to be reminded that You, God is the God of our lives.

a former teenage girl

Psalm 55:22

Cast your cares on the Lord and He will sustain You; He will never let the righteous fail.

Psalm 55:22

Cast your cares on the Lord and He will sustain You; He will never let the righteous fail.

Give You all the "stuff" that worries me? My grades, parents, relationships, clothes, a car. All of my worries. My weight, my appearance! Give it all to You! Or at least I should give it all to You! 'Cast your cares on the Lord' is an invitation to start worrying.

What I consider the meaning of sustained, it means to keep me. It means support. It means to maintain—keep me alive. The context shares that God will support and comfort me if I give my cares to God.

You will never let me fail. I think You will find a way to use my mistakes to Your benefit. You use my issues to expand Your kingdom. Thank You for taking on my cares.

a former teenage girl

Psalm 139:23

Search me, O God, and know my heart; test me and know my anxious

thoughts.

Psalm 139:23

Search me, O God, and know my heart; test me and know my anxious thoughts.

I use the horoscope and other means to understand myself. My friends go to therapists. Others do other things to figure out who they are. But God, You search me and really know me. You know my heart.

God, when I consider what my heart is full of—love, deceit, delight, hurt. My motives are housed in my heart. My vulnerabilities are housed in my heart. My heart is a recovering element.

God, test me and know my anxious thoughts—the things that are on my heart and my mind and cause me to be anxious. Thank You for being concerned about me and my heart.

a former teenage girl

Psalm 139:24

See if there is any offensive way in me, and lead me in the way everlasting.

Psalm 139:24

See if there is any offensive way in me, and lead me in the way everlasting.

God, I could not hide any part of me from You if I wanted to but I want You to correct my offensive ways. I know that I can be disrespectful, rude, mean, deceitful, and lack grace. I know that I am in need of correction.

Ultimately, I would like to be able to handle my issues with as much pleasantry as possible. Sometimes I can but most times I cannot overcome the opposition without being not quite nice.

I am anticipating Your guidance and leadership in my situation. I need some help. I am so easily persuaded to show my discord and behave maliciously. Please help me.

a former teenage girl

Genesis 1:27

So God created man in His own image, in the image of God, He created him.

Genesis 1:27

So God created man in His own image, in the image of God, He created him.

God, You created me in Your image. That was awesome to be able to be the outcome of. God, Thank You for making me like You. When I am doubting myself or am concerned about who I am, then I can reread this scripture.

This is a tall order. With this image, what am I to do? Thank You for giving me an image to keep in mind center which is You. There are some expectations associated with who You are and with whom You expect me to be.

I consider it an honor for such expectations to exist. The daily strides commit me to consider my actions more carefully. Also it requires I consider my image more carefully. When I consider the outcome and the greatness, I am overwhelmed and challenged to uphold Your image.

Mark 14:34

My soul is overwhelmed with sorrow to the point of death. He said to them.

Stay here and keep watch.

Mark 14:34

My soul is overwhelmed with sorrow to the point of death. He said to them. Stay here and keep watch.

Even Jesus got sad. The circumstances will not be like anything we will ever face. You were sad with extreme condition, but awesome outcome and prize resulted. Jesus reminds me that He actually experienced exactly what I do except more intensely and intentionally.

My soul cries for You Jesus and awaits Your comfort. I consider the fact that You have emotions like mine an interesting characteristic. Jesus, You and the Holy Spirit are in consistent communication. Because of this, You respond better than I do. I am working on my emotional responses and outbursts.

I am consistently bargaining for more but I can hear You saying 'stay here and keep watch.' Being still is hard. I am working on it. I am working to be still. Keeping watch is easier because I am observant and understand the magnitude of my duties. Thank You for sharing Your emotions with me.

Mark 14:36

"Abba, Father," He said, "Everything is possible for you. Take this cup from me. Yet not what I will, but what You will."

Mark 14:36

"Abba, Father," He said, "Everything is possible for you. Take this cup from me. Yet not what I will, but what You will."

I do not always get my way either! Jesus, I understand! I do not want some of my responsibilities either although Yours or more important than mine. Jesus, thank You for being my example what to do and how to manage myself.

Daddy, thank You for making everything possible because of You. Thank You for showing me when something is not good for me. Thank You for giving me Daddy in You! I really think that I do not give You enough praise for who You are.

As I better learn to submit to Your will, thank You for showing me Your will. I know that I have broken Your heart before and I am sure that I will again. I am working so hard to know Your will and Your way. I will always seek Your will.

Mark 14:31

But Peter insisted emphatically, "Even if I have to die with you, I will never

disown You." And all the others said the same.

Mark 14:31

But Peter insisted emphatically, "Even if I have to die with you, I will never disown You." And all the others see the same.

I am not sure why Peter said that. We disown You often in our conversation, in our deeds, and in our attitude. Everyday. We deny You when we do something contrary to Your desire.

I will seek to never disown You in my attire or my attitude or my words. I need to seek more of You so that I can be closer to not ever disowning You.

Thank You for not disowning me. I know that I would have disowned me. Help me to better manage so that I do not disown You based on my behavior.

John 13:14-15

¹⁴ Now that I, your Lord and teacher, have washed your feet, you also should wash one another's feet. ¹⁵ I have set you an example that you should do as I have done for you.

John 13:14-15

[14] Now that I, your Lord and teacher, have washed your feet, you also should wash one another's feet. [15] I have set you an example that you should do as I have done for you.

Lord, You have done so much for me as an example for me for how to treat and serve others. I am working to do some every day. I have not actually washed anyone's feet, but I share with small children. I donate clothing to the shelter. I help those who need food by donating food and time to the food bank.

I am working to this serve others the way You show us to serve others by serving us.

As I think of other ways to serve others, I can tutor others, help them apply for college, help them understand You and help current Christians answer questions they may have.

Matthew 14:28-29

[28] *"Lord, if it's you," Peter replied, "Tell me to come to You on the water."*

[29] *"Come," He said. Then Peter got down out of the boat, walked on the water and came toward Jesus.*

Matthew 14:28-29

[28] *"Lord, if it's you," Peter replied, "Tell me to come to You on the water."* [29] *"Come," He said. Then Peter got down out of the boat, walked on the water and came toward Jesus.*

Lord, I have bargained with You before, asking You to prove to me that You were there. You let us walk on the "water" everyday. When we look at our lives, I walked on water when I passed the test. When I spoke in class, I was walking on water. When I won the debate, when I was elected to the Student Council, when I was asked to accompany the speaker on campus, I was "walking on water."

You encourage me to live a life of faith because You continuously offer me opportunities to exercise my faith.

Lord, there are times when I too am overwhelmed by the opportunities You offer me. I could see me in the Peter situation doing the same thing. Sometimes I just get credit for showing up.

Matthew 14:30-31

³⁰ But when he saw the wind, he was afraid and beginning to sink, cried out,

"Lord save me!" ³¹ immediately Jesus reached out His hand and caught him.

"You of little faith," He said, "Why did you doubt?"

Matthew 14:30-31

[30] But when he saw the wind, he was afraid and beginning to sink, cried out, "Lord save me!" [31] immediately Jesus reached out His hand and caught him. "You of little faith," He said, "Why did you doubt?"

God, is that how I behave? Do I get afraid when I have asked for something and You have answered me? I will continuously seek to understand what I request as compared to Your will. I will also consider what I asked for and how You answer me so that I can be prepared to do Your will. I am continuously trying to understand what I can do to better understand Your will.

Thank You for catching me when I fall. Surely I am on my way to failure. You consistently move obstacles from my way so You can be glorified and Your will can be done. I anticipate that I will always try to discern Your will based on what I hear from You.

God, I apologize for doubting. I know my doubt costs me something, inclusive of portions of our relationship. I just don't know how much. I am trying to upgrade my faith. I work on it each day. Some days I am successful. Some days You catch me by the hand.

Romans 8:28

And we know that in all things God works for the good of those who love

Him, who been called according to His purpose.

Romans 8:28

And we know that in all things God works for the good of those who love

Him, who been called according to His purpose.

In ALL things. . . All events. All people. All activities. So even the
evil and bad that happens in my life, God has the ability to have that work
for my good as well. So the hardship that has happened in my life will be
beneficial later.

Even the attempts the enemy makes on my life and my efforts will
be used by You, God, for my good.

This Scripture has some conditional statements: 1) I have to love
God; and, 2) I have to understand my calling according to His purpose. So I
love God. You measure my love by my attentiveness and obedience to You.

I am called according to Your purpose. I am working to understand
my complete purpose for You, Lord. So if I am in my place doing Your
work then, I can count on those things all working together for my good.
God, You will receive the glory at all times when that happens.

In Jesus' name.

♦ 217 ♦

Romans 8:31

What, then shall we say in response to this? If God is for us, who can be

against us?

Romans 8:31

What, then shall we say in response to this? If God is for us, who can be against us?

God, You are for me. You are my Creator. You are my Strength. God, You are my main supporter. God, You are for me! God, You provide me with all types of protection: for my heart, my mind, my soul, and my enemies.

Who can be against us? Everyone will try to be against us. I have a list of enemies. There are people who do not love me because You love me. The ones that hate me because of the gifts You have given me. There are those who try to defeat me because You are invested in me. There are those which try to discourage me because I am focused on You.

God, thank You for keeping my enemies at a distance. Thank You for keeping them unsuccessful while they intend to cause me to fail. God, thank You for keeping me on the alert for my enemies so that I don't get in relationship with the wrong people. Thank You for keeping me safe.

a former teenage girl

Romans 8:37

No, in all things we are more than conquerors through Him who loved us.

Romans 8:37

No, in all things we are more than conquerors through Him who loved us.

In ALL things. In ALL things, You have empowered me to be a conqueror. You have made me more than a conqueror. He has shown me how to conquer the enemy before me. You have destined, determined and designed me to be a winner with a conquering nature.

I am able to overcome my enemies through You because of Your love for me. You love me so You made me a conqueror. You consider my winning a reflection of what You have designed for me.

You love transcends the plot of the enemy. The enemy has no chance against you God. You design our lives such that the enemy had the chance to confront us but only by Your permission and only because You have something to teach us and we will bring You glory with the outcome.

a former teenage girl

IDENTITY CRISIS

By Onedia N. Gage
(Previously published in In Purple Ink: Poetry for the Spirit)

Her words hit me like cold water
Are you mixed
Are you black
I'm black too
Her identity attached to the shallowest of measures
Yet important, extremely

Searching for an identity match
Same shade
Same smile
Same circumstances
Same passion
Searching for the DNA match

Ordinary enough   to fit in
Unique enough   to raise an eyebrow
Distinct enough   to be set apart

No mother near
Mother figure distant in generations
Distant still in relationship

Consistently searching for answers
Countless searches for feedback
Command attention by any means necessary

Just a little time
Answers to questions
From a wondering mind
From a lonely heart

Just some attention
From the right person
Would propel her forward

Don't shed another tear
You will succeed
Just a little help you need

Quit checking for the identity
In ordinary things
Rather start inside

The identity is in her eyes.

HOW GOD DEFINES ME

As my Creator, God defines me as His child. He is my Father! He parents me the best I allow. I consider the parents I have to be stewards according to the will of God.

Even when we do not have parents, God is still our Father. He will send others to serve in that role for what He needs you to have through others.

God has plans for me—Jeremiah 29:11.

As I consider God's definition of me, I am reminded of how He keeps.

I was leaving a job because I did not like it. It was just not what I wanted because I was tired of the aggravation. So I changed jobs from retail to the financial industry. I was studying for the Series 7 exam. I sat for that exam and failed by one percentage point. I am a great test taker. I was devastated. I returned begrudgingly to retail, and eventually to the original retailer I left.

Nine months later, I am awakened by the phone and other end of the phone the voice told me to turn on the television.

I then witnessed one of the most terrible events in US history: the World Trade Center Towers were collapsing. Thousands of lives were tragically ended. EXCEPT ONE: MINE! My life was spared. My life was spared because I failed that test by 1 percentage point. If I had passed that test, I would have been inside those towers and certainly possibly been a part of that tragedy.

God defines me according to His will and according to my obedience. I am defined by His love, His forgiveness, His calling on my life and my obedience to His calling.

He defines me:

Psalm 139:14

John 3:16

Ephesians 4:32

Isaiah 55:8-9

HOW I DEFINE GOD

God is my Creator! I met God and accepted Christ as my Lord and Savior at the age of 6. I was baptized at 6 years old as well. At this level of commitment, I was deeply engaged in ministry. I was eager to served the Lord. I needed the Lord because the storm of my life was starting.

At 12 years old, I challenged the substance of the Sunday School class.

At 16 years old, I was teaching classes at church.

At 27 years old, I was teaching Sunday School to a room of leader's children of which 5 became preachers.

At 28 years old, I was called to preach.

At 33 years old, I answered that call.

At 37 years old, I preached my licensing sermon.

In 2001, I was saved from death by not being there—by not having my own way.

God allows everything that happens to me. God blesses me to live, breathe, and worship Him: God is my God. God is the healer of my ailments. God is the love of my life. God is the light in my darkness. God loves me with the best of Himself. God gives my peace. God shares His vision with me. God gives me courage. God gives me strength. God gives me gifts to use to build the kingdom of God.

God has plans for me and takes care of me. God considers the desires of my heart. God cares for me. I define God as the Being that is Supreme. As a teenager, I define God as a Being that concerns Himself with me.

When I share God with others, I consider how He has met my needs, how He has prepared me for my life, how He has gifted me, and how He has grown me.

I know that when I depend on Him totally is when He is being glorified best. I know that He is my Comforter. He is my Fortress. He is my Source.

HOW I DEFINE LOVE

Jesus dies for my sins because God loves me. I cannot count on human beings, including my parents, to love me with the same magnitude as God, Jesus, and Holy Spirit.

As I defined love for myself so I could decide whether a person loved me, I can use the foundation of God's love. However, we as fragile humans cannot meet the standard of God's love. We do not even love ourselves with the same measure of God.

As I formed my criteria for determining whether you love me, I decided that your behavior will start the measuring of your motives toward me. The criteria: the time you spend with me, the wisdom you share with me, the affection you give, the investment in my interests (do you read my work, do you ask about my progress, do you seek ways to help me succeed, etc.), the forgiveness you give, and the encouragement you give me.

This may not be comprehensive and it is important to understand that this is a high order for some. Sometimes it is hard to me to even reach those criteria. As I consider how I determine that you love me based on the criteria, I measure your effort based on my needs and my effort toward you.

As a teenager, we are presented with so many issues to understand, situations to unravel, concepts to learn, and events to attend. Within the details of all of that, I had decided that I know your love by the consistency of what you do for me and to me.

My love language is quality time. This means that I grade your love based on our time spent. Likewise, trust is a factor—can I trust you with my stuff? I consider you a key player in my life when we spend regular quality time together.

As I grade your love, I consider your contribution to my overall life. If you never ask about my life, then you are not invested in my overall self. When you do not know certain details about me, you clearly do not know me, thus you cannot be defined as loving me.

Finally, when a young man suggests that we become intimate because "he loves me." I have to consider that the measure of his "love" will be compared to that my biological father and then my Creator—Father, Jesus. One gave me life through the participation in my conception. The Other gave me life by His birth, death and resurrection. Their love far exceeds that young man's feeble love offering just so that we can be intimate.

So I define love carefully with great consideration with the criteria for everyone whose paths I cross. I will likewise uphold myself to my definition of love. I will love like I expect to be loved.

HOW I DEFINE IMAGE

As a girl, I was taught to wear slips and girdles and pantyhose. A slip is a polyester 'under-dress' designed to prevent transparency of the dress and keeps the dress from clinging. This slip keeps my body private from the public. The girdle, now known as Spanks, keeps the body parts tight and firmed and shaped. This keeps the dress or pants smooth. This garment helps keep the image of the dress as well. Lastly, the pantyhose keeps the legs smooth as well indicates discretion. The pantyhose adds formality and polish to the dress or outfit.

All of these garments are designed for discretion and polish for my image.

My image is a reflection of my parent's skill set. I am judged by my image. My mother is graded and otherwise blamed for any wardrobe malfunctions.

I recently shared with an older lady and my grandmother that I still wear slips, and pantyhose. They were surprised and excited because this is no longer consistently practiced.

The lack of slips, girdles and pantyhose has been the cause of many wardrobe issues and some information that is not supposed to share with others.

I try to dress and produce an image which makes my family and students proud.

Ultimately, I want to make Christ proud. I want Christ to be pleased with my image because I represent Him. When the public can see through my dress, I put His image in jeopardy. When I do not protect my image, God is at risk.

I define image as how I look when I leave home along with how I live and what I do publicly.

THE NAMES OF GOD

Elohim	The Creator
El Elyon	The God Most High
El Roi	God Who Sees
El Shaddai	The All-Sufficient One
Adonai	Lord, Master
Yahweh	Lord, Jehovah
Jehovah-jireh	The Lord Will Provide
Jehovah-rapha	The Lord That Healeth
Jehovah-nissi	The Lord My Banner
Jehovah-mekoddishkem	The Lord Who Sanctifies You
Jehovah-shalom	The Lord Is Peace
Jehovah-sabaoth	The Lord of Hosts
Jehovah-raah	The Lord My Shepherd
Jehovah-tsidkenu	The Lord Our Righteousness
Jehovah-shammah	The Lord is There
El Olam	The Everlasting God

LEGEND OF BIBLE TRANSLATIONS

KJV—King James Version

NIV—New International Version

MSG—The Message

NKJV—New King James Version

NASB—New American Standard Bible

ESV—English Standard Version

ACKNOWLEDGMENTS

God, thank You for Your plans for me. Thank You for *Love Letters to God from a Teenage Girl* and choosing me to complete Your project. I just want to please You. Thank You for continuing to anoint me and to invest in me and my gifts, which keep surprising me. Thank You for loving and forgiving me.

Hillary and Nehemiah, thank you for your love, enduring my late nights, your ideas, your feedback and advice, and your support. Thank you for loving me, especially when I do nothing without a pen and a clipboard.

To my reading team: The White's, The Randle's, and Ms. Joiner. Thanks for the feedback and the discussions. The bantering has grown me and my writing. Thanks for enforcing the standard and for raising the bar.

To my prayer partners and to my accountability partners, thank you for the long talks and the powerful prayers and the encouragement. Thank you for your presence in my life during this season: Mrs. Kanika Bazzell White and Mrs. Jeanene Wilkinson Holliday.

To the Girls who inspired this work: Brandi, Erica, Jessica, America, Leslie and Jade. May God bless your legacy: strong, bold and transparent.

a former teenage girl

ABOUT THE AUTHOR

Rev. Onedia N. Gage is a girl who was emotionally abandoned at an early age who does not want other girls to go at life alone. She seeks to continue to answer the needs of girls through her activities, published works, speeches, talks and workshops. Rev. Gage is committed to the success of every girl who comes in her path.

a former teenage girl

Lightning Source UK Ltd.
Milton Keynes UK
UKHW011834050620
364530UK00001B/248